A Volcano In My Tummy

Helping Children to Handle Anger

A RESOURCE BOOK FOR PARENTS, CAREGIVERS AND TEACHERS

Warwick Pudney and Éliane Whitehouse

NEW SOCIETY PUBLISHERS

Cataloging in Publication Data:
A catalog record for this publication is available from the National Library of Canada.

Cover design by Warren Clarke.

Printed in Canada.
Thirty-first printing January 2020.

ISBN: 978-0-86571-349-9

First published in New Zealand by the Foundation for Peace Studies Aotearoa, P.O. Box 4110, Auckland, New Zealand, 1994. The Foundation is dedicated to a world without war, and a human race that deliberately chooses reason and negotiation instead of violence and coercion. To this end, it publishes books, works in schools, runs workshops, seminars and conferences, and designs practical programs for learners of all ages to help them change their behavior.

The authors gratefully acknowledge the assistance of the following: Allan King; Colin Whitehouse; John Buckland; Yvonne Duncan; Wendy John; Jim Halliday, and Marion Hancock of the Peace Foundation; Felicity Carter; George Baxter; Paradigm; the schools that trialled this program and, in particular, the staff and pupils of Birdwood School and Colwill School in West Auckland for their valuable feedback; Harper & Collins Publishers; Chatto & Windus Publishers; The Methodist Mission, especially Nola, Acelyn & Silika; and Diana Mumford of Pacific Edge Publishing, Gabriola Island, BC, for her revisions for the North American edition.

Inquiries regarding requests to reprint all or part of *A Volcano In My Tummy* should be addressed to New Society Publishers at the address below.

To order directly from the publishers, please call toll-free (North America) 1-800-567-6772, or order online at www.newsociety.com

Any other inquiries can be directed by mail to:

New Society Publishers
P.O. Box 189, Gabriola Island, BC V0R 1X0, Canada
250-247-9737

New Society Publishers' mission is to publish books that contribute in fundamental ways to building an ecologically sustainable and just society, and to do so with the least possible impact on the environment, in a manner that models this vision. We are committed to doing this not just through education, but through action. This book is one step toward ending global deforestation and climate change. This book is one step toward ending global deforestation and climate change. It is printed on acid-free paper 100% post-consumer recycled (100% old growth forest-free), processed chlorine free, and printed with vegetable-based, low-VOC inks. Additionally, New Society purchases carbon offsets based on an annual audit, operating with a carbon-neutral footprint. For further information, or to browse our full list of books and purchase securely, visit our website at: www.newsociety.com

NEW SOCIETY PUBLISHERS   www.newsociety.com

CONTENTS

INTRODUCTION

My brother said I hit him,
but I didn't.
My father growled at me.
I got mad at my Dad.
When I get angry it's like
I've got a volcano in my tummy.

—A story by L, aged 9.

Children often have problems with anger. Teachers often have problems with anger. Parents often have problems with anger. Why? Because we're afraid of anger. It may mean that someone is out of our control. It may mean that someone won't like us. It may mean that someone acts violently.

This book is about living successfully, healthily, happily, nonviolently, with motivation, without fear and with good relationships.

Put aside your fear and have some fun. This book gives activities, stories, articles, games and learning for all. It is designed for schools and community groups. Parents can easily adapt the lessons for home use. We invite you to use the activities for your children, build them into a program – and enjoy anger!

Specifically, we aim to help children:

- To be aware of when they become angry in the early stages so that they have some choices about what they do with the feeling.

- To distinguish between emotions and behavior.

- To find whether they really need to be angry.

- To learn how to take Time Out and keep safe.

- To learn alternatives to physical and verbal violence and express themselves positively and assertively.

- To take advantage of anger as a motivator for change.

- To identify recycled or dirty anger and personal triggers.

- To discover the ways they have learned to express anger and to choose new ones.

- To learn how to handle other people's anger.

- To develop their self esteem.

- To learn how to deal with authority.

We hope all who use this book will enjoy their anger and benefit from it.

KEY CONCEPTS

➤ Anger is an emotion.

➤ Anger is good, it's healthy, it's normal.

➤ We need anger to protect and motivate ourselves.

➤ Bottled up anger can become explosive, depressive and bad for health.

➤ Violence or abuse is behavior. It can be learned and unlearned. It is not OK.

➤ Violence has many forms—verbal, ethnic/racial, domestic, institutional.

➤ Power or control tactics which frighten people are abuse.

➤ Abuse can be physical, verbal, sexual, emotional or to property.

➤ We are all responsible for stopping violence and abuse.

➤ We need to know what we want and how to ask for it.

➤ Other people's anger is their problem.

➤ Letting others solve their problems is healthy.

➤ Good self esteem means we have less need of anger.

➤ Time Out is for everyone's safety. It stops abuse but doesn't solve the initial problem.

➤ Safe expression of anger is healthy.

➤ Stating what makes us angry is healthy.

➤ We need to learn the words to express our anger in a constructive way.

➤ Learning what triggers our anger makes it easier to control.

➤ Owning our feelings is healthy and reduces conflict.

➤ Behind anger there are feelings of hurt or fear or powerlessness.

➤ We need to know the words to express anger.

➤ We don't always get what we want.

➤ Good listening helps dissipate anger and increase self esteem.

➤ Children learn how to behave from adult models. They learn more from what adults *do* than what they say.

➤ Labelling people is not OK.

➤ Children have rights.

➤ There should be consequences for abuse.

➤ Other people's abuse doesn't have to be accepted.

➤ Parents and teachers have extra power to use justly and responsibly.

➤ Adults and children are fearful of anger because of negative past experiences. It does not have to be so.

➤ Anger rules keep everyone safe.

THE ANGER RULES

> ## The Anger Rules
>
> It's OK to feel angry *BUT*
> - Don't hurt others
> - Don't hurt yourself
> - Don't hurt property
> —*DO* talk about it.

Anger is OK.

Parents too feel angry. Every time we express our own anger positively we give our children a lesson in anger management. As parents, we can help our children by learning to understand our own feelings better.

You might ask yourself some of the following questions:

- How do I react when I get angry?
- How did my parents react when they got angry?
- What happened at my school when someone was angry?
- What did my teachers do when they got angry?
- What did I learn about anger as a child?
- How did I feel as a child around angry adults?
- What do I want my children to know about anger?
- How might they learn this?

> **Anger is a feeling and feelings just *are*.**
> **Anger is OK.**
> **Abuse and violence are *not* OK.**

Somehow, through firm, fair limit-setting, good communication and love, we can let our children know this important message. Every time we do this we contribute to the establishment of a more peaceful society and world.

ESPECIALLY FOR PARENTS AND CAREGIVERS

Being a parent or caregiver can be satisfying and fun. It can also be challenging and frustrating. Children's anger often provides us with a challenge or a dilemma.

- How do we allow our children to express their feelings without being abusive?

- How do we cope with the variety of advice we are offered?

- If we in turn react abusively, our children learn that such behavior is OK.

- We learn what we live. So what can we do to see that all our needs are met?

Children need to learn safe limits to their behavior for their own security and for the safety of others. They also need to know that their feelings are understood.
When this happens a child feels validated and is helped to develop a healthy sense of self.
When setting limits we can use the 'I' statement format on pages 45 and 46.

I feel ....

When (something happens)............

Because ....

I want/would like ....

Or we can be very direct (especially effective for little people).

"We don't hit. Hitting hurts."

"I won't let you hit me. Hitting hurts."

"We don't bite. Biting hurts."

We may need to remove children from the person they are hurting or, if it is us, hold their hands. Eye contact is very effective, but don't force it.

To let children know we have understood their feelings we can offer one of the following:

"It sounds like you're angry."

"Boy, you look furious!"

If we are wrong, our children should have an opportunity to say so.

This kind of communication models for our children a way of coping with their own feelings and provides a vocabulary for doing so. Little children soon learn that what they are feeling has a name. They can use that name to tell people how they feel without acting it out. It also gives children a chance to tell you what their problems are. You might give them a further opportunity by adding:

"And then?" or *"That must be hard"* or *"Tell me some more"* or *"Do you want to tell me about it?"*

Like adults, children do not think too well when they are fired up with anger. They don't listen too well either. It might be better to say:*"We'll talk about this when you are feeling calmer."*
When that happens you might say: *"I want to talk to you about something important. Where shall we go to talk?"*

Then you can use an 'I' statement to express your feelings about the problem and invite your child to suggest a solution.

By the time we reach adulthood most of us have developed methods to stop ourselves going 'over the top' with anger. Children need help to learn this. They may need someone there to say *'Stop'* firmly, or provide the calmness they don't have at that point. In time they will make that control part of their inner wisdom. Until they do they will need yours.

This is particularly true of pre-schoolers who sometimes throw tantrums. Tantrums come about for many reasons, but toddlers are not reasonable when they are having a tantrum. Retaliation just makes them worse. They need an adult to be there to keep them safe and to hold them when it is all over.

Children can be very frightened by the force of their own anger. Parents need a safe way of expressing their own anger about the situation and they need support and someone to talk to – a friend, a parent, a family member, etc. who will support them.

We can often prevent tantrums from happening by child-proofing the environment or organizing our day so that children don't get over-tired and get adequate attention. This is not an easy task for a busy parent. Parenting is hard work. Workers need time off.

Sometimes children are angry with one another. We can assist them at a time like this by:

- stating what we see—*"I see two children fighting over a ball."*

- not taking sides—*"I only know what I see right now."*

- separating the children if there is danger of violence—*"I see someone about to hit someone else. Someone will get hurt. You sit there and you sit there."*

- seeking to find out the reason for the fighting.

Reasons for fighting are many. Children may feel unloved just at that moment. They might feel put down. Or they might be just plain hungry, tired or bored.

Anger can be a positive motivating force:

- Anti-apartheid campaigners in South Africa were angry when they worked to get rid of apartheid.
- Charles Dickens was angry when he wrote to protest about living conditions for the poor in Victorian England.
- William Wilberforce was angry when he worked to abolish slavery.

Key Concepts:
➤ Adults and children are fearful of anger because of negative past experiences.
   It does not have to be so.
➤ Parents and teachers have extra power to use justly and responsibly.
➤ Children have rights.
➤ We need anger to protect and motivate ourselves.

BUILDING CHILDREN'S SELF ESTEEM

Prevention is always the best medicine, and although children's anger should not be dismissed or denied, adults can help to prevent volcano-like explosions of anger by nurturing self esteem in the children they live and work with. With healthy self esteem, children will be more able to handle anger in positive and constructive ways. Here are some suggestions.

1. Children need to be acknowledged for what they are:
   You can do this by what you say:
   - *You're a neat kid.*
   - *I like you.*
   - *I'm glad you're my son/daughter.*
   - *I'm pleased you're in my class.*
   - *I'm glad to see you're back at school.*
   - *Come and tell me about ...*
   - *Come and sit beside me for a while.*
   - *How are you?*

   And do:
   - Make sure they get a turn.
   - Help them individually for a moment.
   - Pat their shoulder as you pass.
   - A smile.
   - Meet their eyes.
   - Remember their name.
   - Ask about something they previously told you

2. Children need to be acknowledged for what they do:
   - *I like the way you finish a job.*
   - *You draw dogs really well.*
   - *That letter 'f' is the best letter on the page.*

3. We need a lot of praise before we can take in criticism without damaging our self esteem. Use the 5:1 rule. One piece of criticism to five pieces of praise or acknowledgment.

4. Don't use generalizations, they are rarely true, e.g. *"You never get to school on time,"* or *"Your work is always messy."*

5. No name calling. Remember labels are sticky, even the seemingly good ones can be harmful. *"You're a good girl"* – a child can infer this means *"I'm only OK when I behave like a little angel."*

6. No put-downs.

7. Don't put unrealistic expectations on children. Get to know the capabilities of children at each stage of development, e.g. adults often say to a child, *"How would you feel if ...?"* Little children don't know, and—it is hard to catch a ball with one hand when you're six!

8. Don't compare one child with another.

9. Criticize the behavior not the child. *"I didn't like what you did,"* instead of *"You're a naughty boy."* The latter puts down the whole child and doesn't leave room for hope. The first means —if I change my behavior things will be better for me.

10. Give children a chance to learn. Behavior doesn't change overnight. Children are in the process of becoming, as we all are.

11. Put yourself on the child's side. *"We've got a problem here. What can we do?"* This gives the child a stake in what's going on.

12. When children feel threatened or frightened they may react with anger. Here are some things children often feel fearful of:
    I might fail.
    I might not be good enough.
    I might not be safe.
    I might not be loved.
    I might be powerless.
    I might not be wanted.
    I might not be liked by other children.
    I might be hungry.
    I might not belong (to family, culture, peer group).
    I might be shown up/embarrassed/shamed.
    I might not understand.
    I might not know the rules.
    I might get hurt.
    I might not know what you want of me.
    I might lose something important.
    I might have something important taken away.

Key Concepts:
➤ Good self esteem means we have less need for anger.
➤ Labelling people is not OK.

WHAT CAN ADULTS DO WHEN A CHILD IS ANGRY?

1. Don't retaliate. (Joining in the child's anger will wind her/him up even more. It will also teach her/him poor ways of resolving conflict.)
2. Model the behavior you want a child to learn. If you hit, s/he learns to hit. If you get out of control, s/he may learn to fear her/his own anger (or teachers, or school, or men).
3. Let her/him know you understand how s/he's feeling. *"I can see how angry you are,"* or *"It seems like you're really mad about that."*
4. Leave explaining another point of view until the anger has been expressed and acknowledged.
5. Ask what s/he would like to do to improve things.
6. Acknowledge what s/he says. Reaffirm the feelings and then help look at the options, e.g. *"What might happen if you did that?"*
7. Don't force children into apologizing when they don't feel sorry. You may be forcing them to bury their anger and be teaching them to be hypocritical.

If two children are angry with each other:
1. Reflect what you see happening. *"I see two children fighting over a ball."*
2. Separate the children if need be for safety's sake. Say, *"Someone might get hurt."*
3. Give them both a way of venting their anger. *"When you've got your anger out, we'll talk about it. You run to the front fence, you run to the back fence and come back to me."*
4. Find out what they each need. *"It looks like you need something to play with."*
5. Find out what they are afraid of. *"Are you worried you won't get a turn if you give him the ball?"*
6. Ask for some solutions.

You can give a child a sheet of paper and say, *"It seems that you're furious. Draw me a picture and show me how angry you are."* Acknowledge the picture. *"I can see you're really mad. What do you want to do with this picture? How are you feeling right now? What might you do the next time you feel as angry as that?"*

If a child has hurt another. Look the offender in the eye and say firmly, *"We don't hit. It hurts."* Attend to the victim and reflect their feelings. *"You were kicked on the leg. I bet that hurts. Draw me a picture and show me how you feel."*

Key Concepts:
➤ Children learn how to behave from adult models.
➤ Children learn more from what adults do than what they say.
➤ Good listening helps to dissipate anger and increase a child's self esteem.

A ONE-TO-ONE ANGER MANAGEMENT PROGRAM

Each one-to-one session (once a week) needs to include a few minutes' talk:

- *Did you feel angry today?*
- *What did you feel like yesterday when …?*
- *When did you feel angry at home this week?*
- *How angry did you feel?*
- *What happened?*
- *What did you do?*
- *Was that a good idea?*
- *Did you stick to the anger rules?*
- *What did … do? (other person)*
- *Was that a good idea?*
- *Did s/he stick to the anger rules?*
- *What are the anger rules?*
- *What could you do to handle this better?*
- *This week I'm going to …*
- *Congratulate yourself for doing … well.*

> ## The Anger Rules
>
> It's OK to feel angry *BUT*
> - Don't hurt others
> - Don't hurt yourself
> - Don't hurt property
> —*DO* talk about it.

- Make a sign for the child to scribble over with colored crayons and display at home.
- Talk about property and what that might include—at home, at school, in the street.
- Talk about how s/he might hurt her/himself.
- Talk about how others might hurt him/her.
- Communication with the family/school is important.

A notebook can go backwards and forwards between home and school and for each day we can make comments, e.g.:

Ripeka was friendly to … today.

Ripeka remembered to stamp her foot when she was angry.

Stephen didn't hurt anyone today.

Stephen hit/kicked … today, but he learned that …

Stickers or stars can go in the notebook. At first this may need to be done two, or even three times a day, but then cut down. Teachers can take this notebook to another teacher or the principal for further praise, comment, or a stamp or sticker.

When the child slips up:
1. Remove him/her from the situation if possible.
2. Allow expression of anger first – *"Punch this cushion (or push my hands or push the wall or tear this paper) and show me how angry you feel."*
3. Reflect how s/he's feeling. *"I can see you feel angry … How do you feel now? … Still angry? … Punch the cushion some more … How do you feel now?"*
4. *"Did you stick to the anger rules? What did you do right? What did you do wrong?"*
5. Don't **make** her/him say s/he's sorry.
6. How can the child help to make things better for …? Do a job for them. Fetch them a drink of water. Share a story book with someone. Pick up some paper so that the room is clean for them. Help with the washing-up. Draw a picture for them. Make them a card. Don't do it (violent behavior) again.

One-to-one activities:
1. Paint and brushes and sheet of paper
   "Show me how angry you felt when … Here's a brush, paper and some paints."
2. Old newspapers
   "When I feel angry I sometimes feel like screwing up newspaper. Use this old newspaper and show me how angry you felt when …"
3. Crayons and paper (newspaper)
   "When I feel angry I sometimes feel like scribbling like this." Demonstrate. *"Show me how angry you felt when …"*
4. Playdough or plasticine
   Get the child to talk about when s/he felt angry at someone (home or school). Get her/him to make the figures with plasticine. You may need to help, e.g. *"Here's how to make a ball for the head, roll a long piece for the legs"* etc. *"Then what do you want to do with these people?"* *"It's not OK to punch, hit or kick the real people."* *"Why not?"* Repeat anger rules. *"But you can squash these little figures."*
5. Puppets
   "This is Sarah."
   (name of the child).
   "This is Uncle Max."
   or *"This is Jo and this is Mom.*
   What are they saying to each other? Show me what they are doing. Show me what they are saying." Alternative: make cardboard and bamboo stick puppets of the characters.

Note: Stress no punishment at home/school.

TROUBLESHOOTING

If you are having problems with anger in your home or class you may like to use these suggestions, but ask yourself these questions first:
• What outlets do children in your room/home have to express their anger?
• Is it OK for children to get angry in your home/class?
• Are you frightened of anger?
• Do you have different values for boys and girls when they express anger?
• Have you negotiated a process for expressing anger with the children in your care? This process will take into account:
      – the children's rights to express their feelings
      – your need to get on with your job
      – your right to express your feelings
      – people's fear of anger
      – respect for others and their property.
• What rights and opportunities do you have to express your anger in your relationships?

Having thought through these issues, the following may be helpful in specific situations.

What to do if: *some useful pages*

1. You find graffiti on the walls 26, 27, 40, 42, 76

2. Children swear in your presence 24, 51, 70

3. You feel like hitting someone 27, 32, 45

4. Vandalism is discovered in the school 26, 27

5. A temper tantrum occurs in your presence 12, 24, 43

6. A child sulks and doesn't want to participate 12, 22

7. A child messes up another's activity or work 8, 12, 43

8. There is name calling in your presence 8, 10, 54

9. A child appears withdrawn 26, 10, 22

10. You have a very 'nice' child who always seeks approval 22, 26, 42

11. A child teases 20, 26, 62

12. A child hurts other children 8, 20, 26

13. You have a child who is a 'poor sport' 42, 43, 70, 72

14. A child tells tales 8, 45

ESPECIALLY FOR TEACHERS

This resource can be used by individual teachers or school staffs to teach anger management skills. It will be used most effectively if the school establishes policy about anger—what is an appropriate expression of anger; how teachers will validate anger; how teachers will handle disputes among children, between adult and child and between staff members; how teachers will encourage children to create change. Parents will need to be informed about the school policy and the anger management program planned for students. The staff may then select age appropriate activities for each class.

It is our wish that this resource be used as fully as possible. To this end, we have aimed to make it as teacher-friendly as possible. Each lesson is clearly explained and worksheets are included that may be photocopied for use with your class.

This resource can be used to run a unit on anger management or it can be used a lesson at a time as the need arises—as a 'first aid' resource when anger-related problems occur.

We have indicated age levels for the exercises. These age levels are suggestions only. Please use your judgement when deciding if an activity is suitable for particular students.

We suggest that teachers read the book right through and do some of the exercises themselves before using the book with children.

IMPORTANT NOTE

Because this resource deals with anger, violence and abuse, it is possible that a child may disclose personal abuse during a lesson. Children who are frequently angry, or especially quiet, may be experiencing physical or sexual abuse. It is important that we, as caregivers, hear and pay attention to deeper reasons for their behavior. Don't ask leading questions (such as, "Is someone ...?" or "are you being ...?") Instead, provide opportunity for the child to talk. *"I notice you have been very quiet lately. Would you like to tell me about it / draw a picture about it? I'm willing to listen and help you"* or *"Show me what you are angry about."* If a child discloses abuse be sure to say you are glad s/he told you. A child may not disclose abuse for a while but the memory of your care and concern will help when s/he does seek help. You should be prepared for this possibility and be clear about your legal responsibility should it occur. We suggest you consult your school administrator and school counsellor before you begin the unit, to plan a process that should be followed.

CURRICULUM INTEGRATION

This resource is specifically for the "Healthy Living" or Social Studies school curriculum. The key concepts can be used as the basis for learning objectives in teachers' lesson plans for these subject areas. However, an integrated anger management unit could be planned using the chart on the following page to select activities in different curricular areas. Learning objectives could then be written to satisfy the Language Arts or Fine Arts curricula as well.

CURRICULUM INTEGRATION

LESSON		Speaking/Listening	Reading	Spelling	Writing	Drama	Art
1	A Volcano In My Tummy (6 yrs. +)	√					√
2	Bottling Anger (9 yrs. +)	√			√		
3	Are You A Volcano? (6 yrs. +)	√			√		
4	The Anger Rules (6 yrs. +)	√					√
5	Dirty Anger/Clean Anger (6 yrs. +)	√			√		
6	Craig's Angry Day (7 yrs. +)	√	√				
7	The Inside Story (7 yrs. +)	√	√				√
8	Technoparent (8 yrs. +)	√	√		√		
9	Time Out (7 yrs. +)	√					
10	Safe Ways of Getting Angry (8 yrs. +)	√			√		
11	Creative Anger (6 yrs. +)						√
12	Tension Scale (6 yrs. +)	√			√		
13	Magic (7 yrs. +)				√	√	
14	Role Playing (8 yrs. +)					√	
15	The Four Levels of Muscle (8 yrs. +)	√			√		
16	Shields (6 yrs. +)	√					√
17	Kalmic and the Angry Alien (8 yrs. +)	√	√		√		
18	Cold Water Words (6 yrs. +)	√			√		
19	Grudge Jar (7 yrs. +)				√		
20	Anger Vocabulary (6 yrs. +)			√			
21	Swearing (6 yrs. +)	√	√		√		
22	Problem Solving (6 yrs. +)	√					√
23	Aggroscenario (9 yrs. +)	√			√		√
24	Anger in the World (10 yrs. +)	√	√				√
25	We Can Make a Difference (10 yrs. +)	√			√		√

RUNNING A STAFF MEETING ABOUT ANGER

If teachers are to use this book fully, it is important that they have an opportunity to discuss and clear any queries or discomforts they have first.

The person leading the meeting could read out the questions below giving teachers time to discuss and think about them. Listen to people's replies, fears and questions and let them know that you understand their concerns, e.g. *"I can see that must be hard for you,"* or *"It sounds like you're really worried about that."*

You may want to say:

"Anger is a feeling. When we talk about our feelings, we talk about part of our inner selves and we need to be sure that anything we say is treated confidentially. We ask you not to discuss people's thoughts outside this meeting. Many of us are fearful of our anger and teachers are no exception."

1. What do you need to know when you hear that there is going to be an Anger Management Program operating in the school?
Discuss this in groups of twos and then share your ideas with the group.
(5 minutes)

2. What are you afraid might happen if the program is used?
Share with the group.

3. Do you feel uncomfortable when children are angry?
What are you afraid might happen?
In twos, discuss and then share with the group. (5 minutes with your partner, 10 minutes group sharing)

Here are some of the fears other teachers have:

- *"I might get physically hurt or the children might."*
  This is a very real fear nowadays. It was our opposition to violence and abuse which prompted us to write this book. One thing to stress throughout is sticking to nonviolent anger rules for everyone.

- *"If I let children express their anger, they might shout and people will think I'm a bad teacher and can't control a class."*
  Maybe the staff could spend part of a future meeting discussing what a 'good teacher' is. Maybe your self esteem is low. If so, you might like to spend some time alone or with a friend or counsellor looking at when and where and how you learned to think badly about yourself.

- *"I don't know why I feel bad when someone shouts, I just do. My stomach knots up."* This might go back to an experience in your past, perhaps forgotten, when someone became angry at you. A counsellor could help you clear this. Looking at our past experiences of anger can help us to understand present fears or discomforts but we may need professional help to clear them completely.

4. What kinds of angry behavior do you find most difficult to deal with?
   List these on a whiteboard. (5-10 minutes)

5. How do you usually react to these? Do you stick to the anger rules?
   Discuss each one with a partner.

6. Does the school have a policy for dealing with angry children?
   Check how the teachers see this policy. Do all teachers know about it? Does it fit in with the
   anger rules or do teachers retaliate with similar behavior to the children? (See: 'What Can
   Adults Do When a Child is Angry?' p. 13)

**7. Does the school, and do the individual teachers, have clear consistent consequences or
   penalties for those who are violent or abusive?**

8. Do these policies need to be changed? How might they be different?
   List on the whiteboard and get someone to note them for future discussion.

The whole meeting should take an hour. If discussion is going beyond time you might want to
schedule a follow-up meeting to go into more depth.

LESSON ONE

A Volcano In My Tummy

Age Level:

6 yrs. +

Teaching Strategy:

Whole class discussion
Individual activity

Key Concepts:

Anger is an emotion.
Anger is good, it's healthy, it's normal.

Materials:

• Pictures of angry people (optional)
• Worksheet – *Do You Have a Volcano In Your Tummy or Explosions in Your Head?*

Procedure:

1. Have your students sit in a circle and briefly review the guidelines for circle discussions.
2. Show a picture of someone who looks very angry (or model an angry person by assuming an angry stance and making an angry face). Ask: *How do you think this person is (I am) feeling? How can you tell?*
3. Discuss the physical manifestations of feeling anger. Ask: *How do you think this person is feeling inside her head? in her stomach? what are her hands doing?* Ask your students to show how they look when they are angry.
4. Discuss the universality of the anger emotion. Ask: *Do you think everyone feels angry sometimes?*
5. Go around the circle so that everyone has a turn to tell what happens to their bodies when they feel angry. Encourage your students to focus on how they *feel* when they are angry, rather than on what they *do*.
6. Wrap up the circle time by writing a class definition of anger. For example: *Anger is an emotion that everyone feels. It's OK to feel angry.*
7. Use the worksheet on p. 21 as an individual activity or ask your students to draw and label a picture of how they look when they are angry. (You may wish to brainstorm a list of words that students will need to label their pictures.)

DO YOU HAVE A VOLCANO IN YOUR TUMMY
OR EXPLOSIONS IN YOUR HEAD?

When we feel angry, things happen to our bodies. Draw what happens to you. Label your picture, e.g. red face

Bottling Anger

Age Level:	9 yrs. +
Teaching Strategy:	Whole class discussion Individual activity
Key Concepts:	Anger is an emotion. Bottled up anger can become explosive, depressive and bad for health. Saying what makes us angry stops bottling. Words can be a constructive way to express anger.
Materials:	• Large glass jar with lid or cork • Small slips of paper to write on • Worksheet – *Bottling Anger*
Procedure:	1. Review the definition of anger written together during the previous lesson.

2. Talk to your students about the difference between emotions and behavior—emotions are feelings, behaviors are actions. Write *Emotions* and *Behavior* on the blackboard and brainstorm words that are appropriate for each heading.

3. Display the large glass jar. Tell your students that one behavior that can result from anger is bottling. Ask what they think that means. Establish through discussion that when people bottle anger they do not express it in a healthy way, but keep it inside.

4. Give each student a slip of paper. Ask them to write something that makes or has made them angry, then crumple the paper and put it in the bottle. Show the bottle full of crumpled bits of paper and discuss what effect having all that anger bottled up inside might have on a person.

5. Discuss a better way to handle anger—stating in words how one feels sometimes helps. Distribute the worksheet on p. 23 and ask the students to write phrases to represent anger they may have bottled up.

Date _____   Name _____

BOTTLING ANGER

Write in the spaces the anger you may have bottled up. Who? When? Where? Why?

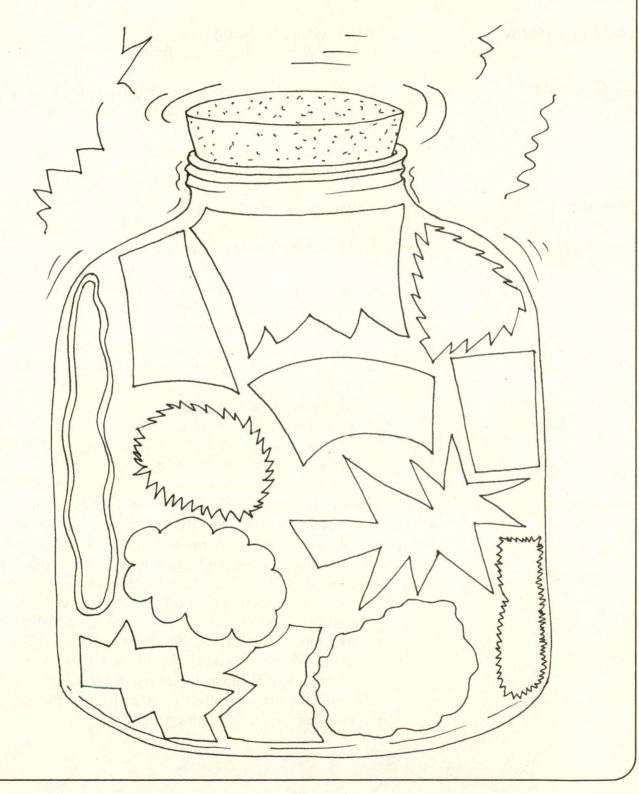

LESSON THREE

Are You a Volcano?

Age Level:

6 yrs. +

Teaching Strategy:

Whole class discussion
Individual or small group activity

Key Concepts:

Power or control tactics which frighten people are abuse.
Abuse can be physical, verbal, sexual, emotional or to
    property.
Violence and abuse is behavior. It can be learned and
    unlearned. It is not OK.

Materials:

• Worksheet – *Are You a Volcano?*

Procedure:

1. Review the key concepts from the previous lessons.
2. Ask whether the students have ever felt frightened by
   someone's anger or have felt their own anger as an
   explosion. Read and discuss the story that inspired
   the title of this resource:

   My brother said I hit him,
   but I didn't.
   My father growled at me.
   I got mad at Dad.
   When I get angry it's like
   I've got a volcano in my tummy.

3. Discuss violent or destructive ways that anger is
   sometimes expressed. What sort of things are said?
   What abusive behaviors are sometimes displayed?
   List all ideas that students suggest. Talk about the
   term *abuse*. Establish through discussion that words
   and behaviors that hurt others or ourselves is abuse;
   that abuse is behavior, not emotion. Establish the
   difference between feeling angry (which is OK) and
   abusive behavior (which is not OK). Discuss the
   damage that is caused by abusive behavior.
4. Distribute the worksheet on p. 25 for completion
   individually or in small groups.

ARE YOU A VOLCANO?

Print words on the flames of the volcano to show what happens during an explosion of anger. Print words on the lava flow to show what damage can result.

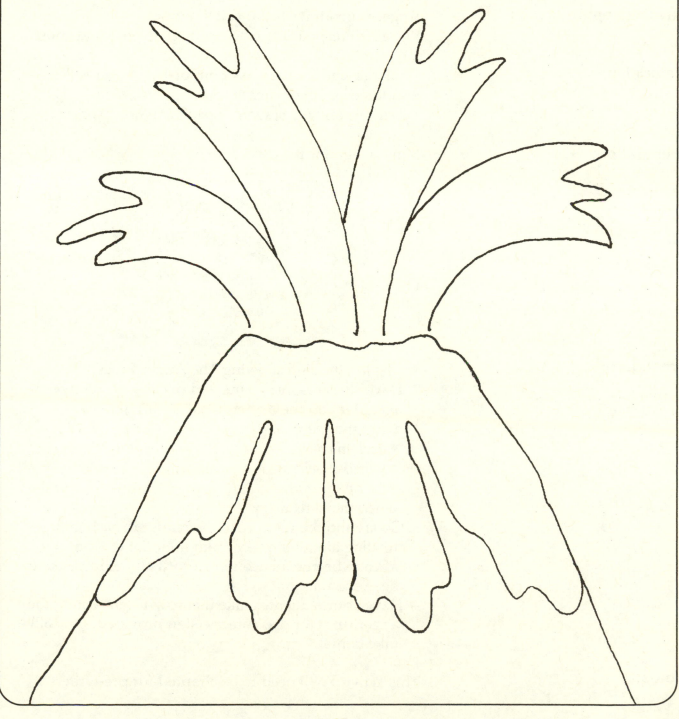

The Anger Rules

Age Level:	6 yrs. +
Teaching Strategy:	Partner activity Individual activity
Key Concepts:	Anger is good, it's healthy, it's normal. We are all responsible for stopping violence and abuse.
Materials:	• A large sign for the classroom of The Anger Rules • Colored paper or card stock • Markers and/or crayons, pencil crayons, paints
Preparation:	Make a sign for the classroom:

> ### The Anger Rules
>
> It's OK to feel angry *BUT*
> • Don't hurt others
> • Don't hurt yourself
> • Don't hurt property
> —*DO* talk about it.

Procedure:

1. Display the sign showing The Anger Rules.
2. Have students form pairs and decide who will be the recorder and the reader in each pair. Ask them to list ways that people:
   • *hurt others*
   • *hurt themselves*
   • *hurt property*
   when they are angry.
3. Go around the room with the reader in each group reading aloud one item from their list that has not already been read. Continue until all the ideas have been shared.
4. Have your students make their own signs listing the anger rules (or decorate the sign provided on p. 80) to take home.

Notes:

This activity will need to be adapted for pre-writers.

Dirty Anger/Clean Anger

Age Level:	6 yrs. +
Teaching Strategy:	Cooperative group activity
Key Concepts:	Anger is good, it's healthy, it's normal. Abuse can be physical, verbal, sexual, emotional or to property. We are all responsible for stopping violence and abuse.
Materials:	• Worksheet – *Clean Anger Is Healthy*
Procedure:	

1. Begin by writing DIRTY ANGER and CLEAN ANGER on the blackboard. Ask your students what clean and dirty anger could be. Through discussion, establish that dirty anger is abusive and clean anger is healthy.
   EXAMPLES OF DIRTY ANGER:
   - kicking doors
   - scribbling on books
   - punching other people
   - writing on desks.

   EXAMPLES OF CLEAN ANGER:
   - angry pushing (door frame, wall, willing adult)
   - running
   - tearing old newspaper
   - punching a pillow
   - writing a letter.

2. Have your students form small groups Have each member of the group assume a role: e.g., chair, recorder, reader, time keeper. Distribute the worksheet on p. 28 to brainstorm strategies for dealing with ways that anger could be expressed cleanly, sticking to the anger rules.

3. After a preset period of time (15 – 20 min.) have the reader of each group read their suggestions aloud. Compile a class list of all the suggestions (eliminate duplicate ideas) to post on the classroom wall.

CLEAN ANGER IS HEALTHY

List ways that you can show clean anger,
sticking to the anger rules.

The Anger Rules

It's OK to feel angry *BUT*
- Don't hurt others
- Don't hurt yourself
- Don't hurt property
—*DO* talk about it.

_____

_____

_____

_____

_____

_____

_____

Craig's Angry Day

Age Level:

7 yrs. +

Teaching Strategy:

Listening or silent reading
Whole class discussion

Key Concepts:

Anger is an emotion.
Anger is good, it's healthy, it's normal.
Bottled up anger can become explosive, depressive and
    bad for health.
Violence and abuse is behavior. It can be learned and
    unlearned. It is not OK.
We are all responsible for stopping violence and abuse.

Materials:

• A copy of *Craig's Angry Day* for each student (optional)

Procedure:

1. Read aloud or distribute copies of *Craig's Angry Day*
    for silent reading.
2. Discuss the following questions:

    1) Where in his body did Craig feel his anger?
    *2) At which points could Craig have stopped his anger
       mounting up?*
    3) What could he have done when it first started?
    *4) Craig was having a conversation in his head with his
       mother and father and teacher. What could he have
       said out loud instead of stewing inside?*
    5) How did Craig break the three anger rules?
    *6) Craig's mother said, "You're just like your father."
       Should she have said that? Why did she say it? How
       did his mother feel when she said it?*
    7) What did you learn from the story?

CRAIG'S ANGRY DAY

Craig and his sister Sarah lived with their mother most of the time, but every second weekend they lived at their father's house. Their mother and father were separated. One morning before school Craig phoned his father.

"Dad, I don't want to come to you this weekend. Can I come next week instead? All my friends are going to the movies this Saturday afternoon."

"No, I'm sorry son, but your Grandma's arranged a family barbecue for Saturday and she especially wants you to be there because she missed seeing you on your birthday. She's baked a cake too."

Craig was angry. He didn't like family barbecues nearly as much as going to the movies with his friends, even if there would be one of Grandma's famous chocolate cakes. "Oh Dad, please. They won't really mind if I'm not there."

"No Craig, you're coming and that's final. Now I've got to go. I'm late for work." His father hung up. Craig slammed the phone down hard.

"Hey, mind that phone," shouted his mother. Craig spun round and kicked out at the back door, but his foot missed the wood and went through the glass panel, shattering pieces of glass outside on to the porch. His mother came running out when she heard the noise.

"Look at what you've done! You'll get yourself into trouble one day with your temper. You can pay for the new glass with your pocket money. Now clean up the glass. You're just like your father."

Craig hated to hear his mother say things about his father. He felt really bad when she talked about his bad temper as though it was a rotten part of him. But he kept quiet and cleaned up the glass. He was boiling inside and his chest felt ready to burst. He slung his school-bag over his shoulder and set out for school.

He was boiling with anger when he pushed with clenched fists through a group of younger children on the footpath. He didn't intend to knock over little Toss. He liked Toss. Toss lived next door and thought Craig was a big hero. Toss had just started school and now he was lying on his back in the gutter crying because his new school bag was muddy. Craig hauled him up roughly and marched on to school.

By math time he wasn't boiling with anger but he was so busy going over in his head what he wanted to say to his mom and dad that he wasn't concentrating on his work. "Craig, you've got every answer wrong today. What's wrong?" asked the teacher. Craig felt his anger bubbling up again. He took his pen and scribbled across his book. The teacher was angry now.

"You can spend recess sitting on the seat by the principal's office doing your math," she said. Now the conversations in his head included his teacher. When lunch-time came Craig was feeling grumpy and hungry. He had stormed out of the house that morning and forgotten his lunch. He climbed to the top of the adventure playground climbing frame. He wanted to be on top and in charge, somewhere where no one could boss him around. But Henare was on top of the tower.

"It's my turn up there now," said Craig.

"I got here first," said Henare.

"Get down," said Craig.

"Make me," said Henare.

So Craig pushed him, but Henare was stronger. Craig felt himself over-balancing. He grabbed wildly for something to hold on to, but there was nothing there. The next thing he knew he was on the ground and his head and shoulder were hurting. Children were crowding around him but their voices seemed far away. He heard his teacher say "I've tried to phone his mother but she's out on a job. So his father's coming to meet us at the hospital. The ambulance will be here soon, Craig." He closed his eyes.

Later that day he lay on the sofa at home with his arm in a sling and his head aching. His dad sat opposite him. His mother had just come in from work. "What happened?" asked his mother. Craig explained about the fall. "You were very mad when you left this morning," said his mother. "Have you told your dad about the hole in the back door?"

Craig turned his head away. His dad looked upset. He stood up and looked out the window.

"You know I used to do things like that when I was angry," he said. "Your mother will tell you. We would have been together today if I had learned to control my anger."

"That's for sure," said his mother. His dad went on. "And you wouldn't have learned these bad habits. So I guess it's my job to teach you some new ones. Lately I've been going to an anger-management course and I've been learning to control my anger. The main thing is to learn the anger rules."

"It seems like you broke all the rules today. But we won't talk any more now. You need to rest. We'll talk at the weekend. It's a pity about the broken collar-bone. Grandma was hoping you'd mow the lawns on Saturday." He grinned as he walked out.

The Anger Rules

It's OK to feel angry *BUT*
- Don't hurt others
- Don't hurt yourself
- Don't hurt property

—*DO* talk about it.

The Inside Story

Age Level:

7 yrs. +

Teaching Strategy:

Whole class: listening or silent reading
Individual activity

Key Concepts:

Anger is an emotion.
Anger is good, it's healthy, it's normal.
Violence and abuse is behavior. It can be learned and
    unlearned. It is not OK.
We are all responsible for stopping violence and abuse.
We need anger to protect and motivate ourselves.

Materials:

• A copy of *The Inside Story* for each student (optional)
• Strips of paper for signs
• Crayons, pencil crayons, markers

Procedure:

1. Read *The Inside Story* aloud or distribute copies for
    silent reading.
2. Ask your students to think of a saying for themselves
    to help them stop and think before reacting in anger.
3. Allow time for the students to make and decorate a
    sign showing their sayings.

THE INSIDE STORY

Many years ago our ancestors had to fight to survive. They didn't know any other way. Maybe someone had stolen their food or taken their home. Anger was important to them. It helped them to stay alive. When they got angry, their bodies made them ready to attack. Fear helped them to run away if the situation was too dangerous.

Nowadays, your body works in the same way when you are angry or scared. Your body releases hormones, or "messengers," into your bloodstream. These hormones tell your body to be prepared for "fight or flight." Next time you are angry, feel your body waking up and getting ready. What happens in your hands, face, chest, stomach?

One important part of your body that gets 'anger' messages is your brain. Part of your brain makes your body aware of how you are feeling. But there are other parts of your brain which do the thinking. Many of us act angry. As soon as we feel angry we punch, hit, kick and yell words at each other. If we take our anger to the thinking parts of our brain first we can think of better things to do. We can think of less harmful things to do with our fists and feet and words.

This is why we hear old sayings like "count to ten when you get angry." Counting to ten helps you to think before you act. Once you have taken the message to the thinking center of your brain you can remember the anger rules. You could make up your own saying to remind you to think first. Write your saying on a sticker and decorate it. Wear your badge at home and show it to your mom and dad. Or you could make a sign for your kitchen or classroom.

Some people store up their anger instead of letting it out in good ways. When they store up their anger, the hormones (messengers) keep going round and round in their bodies and the people get sick. Other people have problems because they keep a small amount of anger smoldering away for a long time and every now and then it flares up. It's a bit like having a fire burning low for a long time. People come along and stoke it or put another log on and it flares up. Burning with anger for a long time uses a lot of energy and can make us sick or unhappy.

Technoparent

Age Level:	8 yrs. +
Teaching Strategy:	Listening or silent reading Whole class discussion or individual activity
Key Concepts:	We need to know what we want and to ask for it. Violence or abuse is behavior. It can be learned and unlearned. It is not OK. Other people's anger is their problem. Good self esteem means we have less need of anger. We are all responsible for stopping violence and abuse.
Materials:	• copies of *Technoparent* (optional) • Worksheet – *Technoparent*
Procedure:	1. Read *Technoparent* aloud or distribute copies for silent reading. 2. Discuss the questions on the worksheet on p. 37 orally or distribute copies for written responses.
Extension:	Students may enjoy writing their own stories about Brian's invention.

TECHNOPARENT

Terry kicked his friend's bedroom door open and ran and landed on his bed with a leap that crunched the mattress. "Whatcha doing, Nerdbrain? Come on outside and throw rocks."

"I've got it. I've got it. It's finished," said Brian (alias Nerdbrain).

"What? What have you got, Megahead?" replied Terry impatiently.

It was a pain having a technogenius as a friend except when you wanted to cheat at computer games. "Technoparent. The hand-held parent. No longer will you need a parent to tell you when you're doing something wrong. No longer will you have to take all that boring advice from your mother or father. This does it all, Terry old pal. The replacement for smart parents," said Brian.

"You're joking. That's just an old calculator. You're talking rubbish again, Burphead." Terry often called his friends names. Immediately the pocket calculator lit up in Brian's hand with colored flashing lights.

"It's working, it's working. Let me press 'total' and see what it's picked up." Brian was excited. This was a test run. He had packed all known speeches made by parents on T.V. in the last year on to the micromemory, plus a few he had taped when his father was in a bad mood. The calculator flashed again and they both peered at the tiny screen.

"TERRY CALLED BRIAN A BURPHEAD BECAUSE TERRY FEELS DUMB SOMETIMES WHEN BRIAN INVENTS THINGS. HE IS AFRAID OF BEING A NOBODY. HE WANTS BRIAN TO BE A NOBODY TOO. HE NEEDS TO SAY THAT HE ADMIRES BRIAN'S BRAINS."

"What a stupid, smartmouth machine. Let me smash it, Bonkbrains," Terry said, going an embarrassed red. The calculator flashed again.

"TERRY IS ANGRY BECAUSE I TOLD THE TRUTH. HE NEEDS TO SAY IT'S TRUE AND THAT TERRY, HIMSELF, IS A GREAT PERSON AS WELL AS BRIAN."

"That's right, I am a great person. Did you hear that, Brian? This machine's OK. Can I borrow it?" said Terry, relieved.

"Seeing you're a great person, you can borrow it for today, but bring it back," replied Brian, relieved to not be called a name for once.

Terry had already gone through the door, without kicking it for once. He raced down the road towards his home so fast that he ran into Matilda, a girl in his class, as she came out of her gate. "Sorry," she said, as she picked herself up from the hedge bush.

"Yeah. Why don't you look where you're going, Frogeyes," he said, nursing his chin. Immediately the calculator in his hand flashed green as if it had frog eyes.

"TERRY WAS EXCITED AND WASN'T LOOKING WHERE HE WAS GOING. HE BLAMED MATILDA. HE IS AFRAID OF LOOKING SILLY AND BEING A NOBODY. HE NEEDS TO SAY IT WAS HIS FAULT AND THANK HIMSELF FOR BEING BRAVE AND HONEST."

Terry stammered. "S-s-sorry. I wasn't looking where I was going."

"That's fine! Great computer game. See ya," said Matilda, and danced off down the road. Terry felt funny. He felt quite good down inside himself and that was unusual. Mostly he felt sort of scary and angry inside and he just pretended to be fine by calling people names and bossing them. But right now he felt sort of brave and pleased inside.

"Great computer game, TECHNOPARENT!" he thought. "I must try this out on the kids down at the spacey alley." He raced off and soon arrived, panting, at the darkened alley with a thousand flashing lights inside.

"Look who's here. It's Cabbageface." A

voice from inside called out loud enough for everyone to notice it. It was Steve, the kid from around the corner who seemed to like to tangle with Terry. He stood there sneering at Terry who was just puffing himself up and thinking of the worst things to call him back when Technoparent flashed off in his hand.

"HE'S REALLY JUST PRETENDING TO BE BIG LIKE YOU DO. YOU DON'T HAVE TO HIT BACK. TELL YOURSELF THAT YOU'RE NOT A CABBAGEFACE BUT THAT YOU ARE A BRAVE AND GOOD PERSON. PASS HIM A COMPLIMENT."

Terry paused a moment and replied "Hi, Steve. How's the game going? Still scoring high?"

Steve looked amazed. This was the first time that Terry had ever not hit back with his words. He tried again. "Whaddaya mean, Trashhead?"

"DON'T TAKE THE BAIT," said Technoparent.

"I'm feeling great to-day. How'ya going, Steve?"

Steve slunk back into the dark of the games alley with a confused look on his face. Terry wasn't supposed to feel great if he wasn't. Terry felt even better than before. He slipped Technoparent back into his pocket and walked off thoughtfully towards home. As he pushed open the front door, he heard his mother and father arguing in the kitchen. He hated his parents arguing. They were often doing it. He felt like kicking doors when they argued. He was about to give his bedroom door an almighty boot when he felt Technoparent flash in his pocket.

"YOU ARE AFRAID YOUR PARENTS WILL SPLIT UP AND YOU WILL BE UNLOVED AND FORGOTTEN. DON'T HIT BACK AT DOORS OR PEOPLE—TELL THEM."

"Are you joking?" he thought. Then he thought "Why not?" He sat down and got out a pen and paper. He wrote:

Dear Mom and Dad,

I hate it when you argue all the time. I feel afraid that you will split up and I won't have a home and I'll be forgotten. Sometimes it feels as if you take your problems out on me. I wish you'd stop.

Love, Terry

He put Technoparent under his pillow, folded the letter and went downstairs. He paused before entering the kitchen. He heard his dad talking,"... and you've got to stop wasting money on things we don't need. We can't afford all your pretty bits and pieces. My hours at work have been cut and we don't have the money anymore ..."

Terry opened the door and walked in. Something went click in his head.

"DAD, YOU'RE BLAMING MOM. YOU'RE REALLY FEELING BAD ABOUT NOT EARNING ENOUGH MONEY FOR EVERYONE AND YOU'RE AFRAID IF YOU DON'T DO YOUR JOB PROPERLY YOU'LL BE A NOBODY. YOU NEED TO SAY JUST THAT AND TALK WITH MOM ABOUT HOW WE CAN MANAGE. YOU NEED TO TELL YOURSELF THAT YOU ARE A GOOD PERSON AND A GOOD DAD."

Terry put his letter on the table, turned and walked out. He couldn't believe he had said that. Wow! He ran to the phone and called Brian. Brainy Brian!

"Hey Brainy, hey Brian. It works. It's fantastic. And I don't need it anymore. I can do without Technoparent. It just happens in my head. I'm the TECHNOKID. Wowee!"

TECHNOPARENT

1. Why did Terry go around calling people names?

_____

2. Think of a time when you called someone a name. What could you have said
   instead about how you truly felt inside? Be brave and honest like Terry.

_____

3. What are six good names you can call your friends? Make them compliments like
   "Brainy Brian."

_____

_____

4. What would you reply if somebody called you "Cabbageface"?

_____

5. How do you feel when your parents fight?

_____

6. Why do you think Terry kicked doors?

_____

7. What's the best compliment you can think of for yourself?

_____

8. How can this story help you?

_____

9. If you could invent something to help your friends, what would you make?

_____

10. Write a letter to one or both of your parents to tell them something that you
    are unhappy about.

LESSON NINE

Time Out

Age Level: 7 yrs.+

Teaching Strategy: Class discussion
Individual or small group activity

Key Concepts: Time out is for everyone's safety. It stops abuse but doesn't solve the initial problem.

Materials: • Worksheet – *Time Out*

Procedure:

1. Most students know the hand signal for "Time Out" used in sports. Discuss what it means and when it is used. Time Out can also be used as an anger management tool. It is useful for controlling anger and for giving ourselves time and space to think about safe ways of resolving problems. It is not a form of punishment. Ask: *How could "time out" help when someone is angry at home or at school? What could the angry person do during his Time Out to handle his feelings in a healthy way?*
2. Distribute copies of the worksheet on p. 39 to individual students or small groups to complete.
3. Compile a class list of Time Out strategies from the responses recorded on the worksheet.
4. Adopt the Time Out hand signal for use by you and your students when conflicts arise in the classroom.
5. Establish a Time Out chair/place where a student can go when s/he can't handle being near other people. Ask students to use the Time Out chair when they feel like breaking the anger rules. Direct students to the Time Out chair if necessary. Encourage students to express their anger: *I am mad. I am going to sit on the Time Out chair.* Perhaps make art materials available so that anger can be expressed visually. Make it clear that students are welcome to rejoin the group when they no longer feel angry enough to break the anger rules. Discuss ways to solve the problem that caused the anger.

TIME OUT

What could you do to CALM DOWN and keep out of trouble?
Go through the Time Out doors and fill in the spaces with your ideas.

Safe Ways of Getting Angry

Age Level: 8 yrs. +

Teaching Strategy: Individual or small group activity

Key Concepts: Violence and abuse is behavior. It can be learned and
unlearned. It is not OK.
Safe expression of anger is healthy.

Materials: • Worksheet – *Safe Ways of Getting Angry*

Procedure:

1. Review the ways of expressing anger that have been
identified and discussed in previous lessons.
2. Distribute copies of the worksheet on page 41 to small
groups or individual students.
3. After 15 or 20 minutes, ask each student to read one
idea from his paper that has not already been read.
Continue until all ideas have been shared.

Possible responses:
• tell others how you feel
• tell the person what you would really like
• complain
• figure out peaceful ways of changing things
• write down how you feel
• show people what they've done, hurt or damaged
• talk to someone
• start a petition
• write letters
• do something physical
• get support of other people.

Date _____   Name _____

SAFE WAYS OF GETTING ANGRY

Fill in with your own ideas

Creative Anger

Age Level:	6 yrs. +
Teaching Strategy:	Individual activity
Key Concepts:	Safe expression of anger is healthy.
Materials:	• crayons, paints, markers • colored paper • magazines to cut up • yarn and fabric scraps
Procedure:	1. Discuss how art can help release emotions. 2. Invite your students to express their anger about something in their lives by creating a picture or collage using a variety of materials. 3. Invite your students to talk about their pictures in a circle discussion format.
Suggestions:	1. Draw the angriest face you can think of. 2. Some people say that they feel like they have a fire or volcano inside when they are angry. Paint a fiery picture to show how you feel. 3. Use magazines to find colors that express your anger. Make a collage of small pieces of colored paper.
Option:	A large sheet of paper could be provided for graffitti art. This needs to be posted where people can come and paint, draw or write when they get angry.
Notes:	Useful phrases for adults to help children express and talk about anger: *I bet there's a special story for this picture.* *If there was a special story for this picture, what would it be?* *I'm guessing this was a time that you were really angry.* *When was the last time that you were angry like that?* *This bit is really interesting. Tell me about it.* *I notice . . . Can you tell me about . . .?*

Tension Scale

Age Level:

6 yrs. +

Teaching Strategy:

Whole class instruction
Discussion with a partner

Key Concepts:

Learning what triggers our anger makes it easier to
   manage.

Materials:

• Worksheet – *What Lit the Fuse?*

Procedure:

1. Introduce the idea of a tension scale which measures
the intensity of angry explosions. Draw a ten point
ladder or thermometer on the blackboard and, as a
group, name each point on the scale. Teach your
students that the tension scale can be used to calm
themselves when they are very angry using the
following technique:

Breathing Down the Tension Scale

*1) Picture the tension scale in your head. It may
help to close your eyes.*
*2) Think about how angry you are. Is your anger a
six or an eight, a five or a nine?*
*3) Now take a deep breath. Breathe out very
slowly.*
*4) As you breathe out, picture your anger coming
down the Tension Scale.*
*5) When your anger is at a safe level, think about
how you might resolve your problem.*
*6) Congratulate yourself for using good anger
management.*

---

2. Use the worksheet on p. 44 to start your students
thinking about what triggers their anger, or causes
angry explosions.

WHAT LIT THE FUSE?

If we are stressed, worried or carrying anger around, it may only take a little thing to trigger an explosion. Everyone has different triggers, e.g. being called a particular name. What things particularly annoy you? A particular person? Being bossed? Unfair things? List four of them below.

1. _____   3. _____

2. _____   4. _____

Write down a situation in which you exploded over a little thing.

_____

_____

Discuss the situation with a partner. Ask each other these questions:
   1) How high on the Tension Scale did you get?
   2) Who did you show your anger to?
   3) Who were you really angry with?
   4) How did you feel inside your body?
   5) What did you do with your body?
   6) What was your trigger?
   7) What did you do to get control of your anger?
   8) Did you direct it (use it wisely), repress it (bottle it) or explode?

Magic

Age Level:

7 yrs. +

Teaching Strategy:

Role playing

Key Concepts:

Stating what makes us angry is healthy.
Owning our feelings is healthy and reduces conflict.

Materials:

• Worksheet – *Want Some Magic to Help You?*

Procedure:

1. Ask a student to role play with you to demonstrate the difference between "I" statements and "you" statements. Give the student a scenario to act out in which he/she says something that could trigger anger. You may wish to tailor the scenario to something relevant to what goes on in your particular class, e.g., name calling, racial slurs, bullying, put downs.
2. Respond with a "you" statement the first time to demonstrate how an argument escalates. Then re-enact the entire scenario, but this time respond with an "I" statement.
3. Discuss what kind of information should be conveyed in an "I" statement: how you feel, what triggers that feeling and what you want to happen or change.
4. Use the worksheet on p. 46 as a follow up.

WANT SOME MAGIC TO HELP YOU?

- Use 'I' statements to say how you feel and what you want.
- Never use 'You' statements because people think you're blaming them.

Learn this by heart – this is magic!

| I feel _____ (angry, annoyed, furious, niggled, etc.) |
| when _____ (say what happened) |
| because _____ (why it upsets you) |
| I would like _____ (what you want to happen or change) |

Think of 2 situations in which you felt angry with someone.
Using the 4-part magic phrase, write what you could have said in those situations.

1. (a) I feel _____

   (b) when _____

   (c) because _____

   (d) I would like/prefer/want _____

2. (a) I feel _____

   (b) when _____

   (c) because _____

   (d) I would like/prefer/want _____

Role Playing

Age Level:	8 yrs. +
Teaching Strategy:	Role playing
Key Concepts:	Anger rules keep everyone safe. Stating what makes us angry is healthy.
Materials:	• Role play instructions • Role play situations on strips of paper

Procedure:

After working through the Magic strategy in Lesson 13, divide your students into small groups to role play the scenarios on the following pages. Distribute a copy of the instructions to each group.

OPTIONAL

Instead of supplying the scenarios, start by asking your students to write scenarios of situations that would make them angry. Put all the suggestions into a box and have each group draw one to act out.

Role Play Instructions

In groups of 3 or 4 make up a mini-play of what you would do if these things happened.

Put on your play to the class and then ask the others to tell you if they think the angry person handled the situation in a healthy way.

Remember the anger rules and the Magic 'I' Statements when you make up your mini-play.

Your solutions need to include a way of safely expressing feelings and, if need be, sorting out the problem. You can do these by saying what you need and what you're scared of and then listening to the other person.

1. What would you *do* if you come home from school and find your brother and his friend playing in your room with the new game you just got for your birthday? Your mom is in the kitchen.

----

2. What would you do if your friend is at your house playing and asks you to stay the night at his house but your mom says, "No"?

----

3. What would you do if you come home and find your dad cooking supper and he is making stew again and you had stew the night before, and you think stew is the yuckiest meal ever?

----

4. What would you do if you are about to go out with the class to play softball on a warm summer afternoon and the principal comes into your class and says, "I need two helpful people to clean out the phys. ed. cupboard," and she chooses you?

----

5. What would you do if you go to get the new pencil your aunt gave you with the alligator's head on the top and someone's taken it from your desk?

----

6. What would you do if you're playing with your brother, and your mom tells you that your dad just phoned to say you can't go to his house this weekend and he had told you he would take you to the fun park on Sunday?

----

7. What would you do if you planned to meet your friends on Saturday at the shopping mall and your mom says you have to stay home and look after your younger brothers and sisters while she goes to the hospital clinic?

----

8. What would you do if you were wearing your new sweat shirt Uncle Ray sent from Australia with a koala on the front and someone spills their orange juice down it at lunchtime?

----

9. What would you do if you are about to leave for school, you say goodbye to your mom and dad and turn round to pick up your big project about the solar system and you find that the cat has walked over it and left muddy footprints?

----

10. What would you do if you did the dishes last night and now your mom and dad are saying it's your turn tonight, and your sister's grinning and you know that she knows it's her turn?

----

11. What would you do if your neighbor stopped you from taking a short-cut across his yard so you could catch up with your friends out on the street?

----

12. What would you do if Grandma came by this afternoon and left a big piece of chocolate birthday cake and your mom says you and your brother can have half each and your brother's going to cut it, and you know your brother doesn't know about fractions and he's going to give himself a much bigger piece than you?

---

13. What would you do if your mother can't afford to give you money for the class trip because she needs all her spare money to pay for some medicine for your sister and brother?

---

14. What would you do if there are two boys in your class who never put the soccer balls away at recess, and the teacher gets mad one day and says, "Right. Nobody will use the soccer balls at recess all this week and then maybe you will learn to put them away"?

---

15. What would you do if your brother is playing football and he kicks the ball into your mom's prize rose bush and breaks it and runs off. But you come round the corner and your mom thinks it was you and she says, "You're a clumsy kid. You can just pay for that out of your pocket money"?

---

16. What would you do if the storekeeper accused you of taking some chocolate bars when you saw some other boys shoplifting a few minutes earlier?

The Four Levels of Muscle

Age Level:

8 yrs. +

Teaching Strategy:

Instruction
Individual or small group activity

Key Concepts:

Stating what makes us angry is healthy.
Owning our feelings is healthy and reduces conflict.

Materials:

• Transparency of *The Four Levels of Muscle*
• Worksheet – *Using Your Muscles*

Procedure:

1. Discuss the four levels of muscle as outlined on the next page (make a transparency of this page for the overhead projector).
2. Work through one or two scenarios on the worksheet on p. 53 with the whole group. Assign the rest of the scenarios as individual or small group work.

Notes:

Pamela Butler, in her book *Self Assertion for Women*, wrote about using "levels of muscle" for asserting ourselves when we feel put down, helpless and angry. We have adapted these for children's use. A method such as this gives children power. Without victims, the bullies can't continue. It also helps children to learn that behavior has consequences.

THE FOUR LEVELS OF MUSCLE

LEVEL 1 MUSCLE – THE 'I' MESSAGE

Give an 'I' message. State clearly how you feel and how you want things to be different. Look the person in the eye when you speak.

"When my work is copied I feel angry. I want you to do your own work."

LEVEL 2 MUSCLE – GETTING STRONGER

Restate your 'I' message with more emphasis.

"I said, when my work is copied I feel angry. I mean it."

LEVEL 3 MUSCLE – STATE CONSEQUENCE

Restate your 'I' message and say what you will do if the annoying behavior does not stop. When you make a threat it must be one you can carry out and will carry out.

"I said, when my work is copied I feel angry. I want you to do your own work. If you do it again, I will tell the teacher; I mean it."

LEVEL 4 MUSCLE – FOLLOW THROUGH

Restate your message and follow through—do what you said you would do.

"I told you not to copy my work. I said I would tell the teacher and that's what I'm doing right now."

USING YOUR MUSCLES

A. In the playground at lunchtime, a classmate who is not playing with you and your
   friends keeps interrupting and calling you names.

Level 1 _____
Level 2 _____
Level 3 _____
Level 4 _____

B. At home in your bedroom, your brother or sister is teasing you and won't give
   back something of yours.

Level 1 _____
Level 2 _____
Level 3 _____
Level 4 _____

C. At a friend's house with two other friends who are also visiting, one friend has
   had far too long on a computer game and it's your turn.

Level 1 _____
Level 2 _____
Level 3 _____
Level 4 _____

D. At home watching television, your brother turns the TV to a different channel in
   the middle of your program.

Level 1 _____
Level 2 _____
Level 3 _____
Level 4 _____

E. Walking home, a strange man asks you if you want a lift.

Level 1 _____
Level 2 _____
Level 3 _____
Level 4 _____

LESSON SIXTEEN

Shields

Age Level:	6 yrs. +
Teaching Strategy:	Whole class discussion Individual activity
Key Concepts:	Abuse can be verbal, sexual, emotional or to property. Owning our feelings is healthy and reduces conflict. Other people's abuse doesn't have to be accepted.
Materials:	• Shields or pictures of shields • Worksheet – *Shields*
Procedure:	1. Bring a real shield to class if you have access to one, or show pictures of shields from books and magazines. Discuss the purpose of shields and how they are decorated. 2. Ask your students to think about things that do or could shield them from hurtful words or actions, angry people, fearful things. These shields may be tangible objects, or images or ideas. 3. Distribute copies of the worksheet on p. 55.

OPTIONAL

Use the worksheet as a planning tool for students to plan a larger shield to be hung on the wall.

SHIELDS

Draw yourself a shield that can protect you. You may draw on it things that help you feel happy and safe. It can be old fashioned, new, science fiction. It can have special equipment on it. It may need words. It needs to be colored. Explain how it works to protect you.

_____

_____

_____

_____

_____

_____

Kalmic and the Angry Alien

Age Level:

8 yrs. +

Teaching Strategy:

Listening or silent reading
Class discussion or individual or group activity

Key Concepts:

Bottled anger can become explosive, depressive and bad for health.
Power and control tactics which frighten people are abuse.
Behind anger are feelings of hurt, fear or powerlessness.

Materials:

• *Kalmic and the Angry Alien*
• Worksheet – *Debrief*

Procedure:

1. Read *Kalmic and the Angry Alien* aloud or distribute copies for silent reading.
2. Discuss the questions on the worksheet on p. 60 with the whole class or assign for individual or small group completion.

KALMIC AND THE ANGRY ALIEN

Kalmic struggled awkwardly into the official uniform of the Intergalactic Life Research Foundation. "Do I have to wear this?" she complained, and stood with her arms outstretched, the long sleeves hanging down past the ends of her arms. Being an expert on alien life forms at age nine has its problems. No one seems to believe you for a start and they certainly don't make uniforms your size.

"Oh forget it, take it off," said Commander Polk. "It's more important to get you on the job. I'll check you through security." Still in her tracksuit, Kalmic, the child expert on alien life forms, was shown into the center hall of Alien Research by the Commander. Uniformed scientists busied themselves at tables and around the walls were large glass windows, many with strange and unusual shapes, peering quietly out at their captors. "What's she doing here? Kid's out!" boomed a voice.

Kalmic and the Commander turned. Behind them stood a tall, red-faced military man. "Captain Aggrow, meet Kalmic the cosmic kid, expert on alien life and here by order of the government to assist on life-form RAD 33," said Commander Polk, in a crisp voice.

"A kid! We've had my team of intergalactic bio-geneticists working on the case for a month without results, and you bring me a kid! What do you think I am? I haven't worked here for 3 gryptons to be made a fool of. Take her back to school," said the Captain, his voice getting louder and faster.

"No choice, Captain. By order of the Institute and the Minister, you are to assist her in every way. Is that understood?" said the Commander. Kalmic looked up at Captain Aggrow as he spluttered, went another shade of red and looked as if he was going to burst his uniform. She quietly smiled and saluted him and put out her hand in welcome.

The Captain struggled, then quickly shook her hand and said "Hmmph. You'd better come with me."

Kalmic followed the Captain to a group of scientists. "These are the team who know what they have to do. This kid here's supposed to help. Come and see RAD 33," said Captain Aggrow in a sharp voice. He strode into a separate room with a large window and pulled the screen aside. He banged on the huge wall of glass with a measuring rod. Immediately a large jelly-like creature lunged at the glass. Its six huge flaming red eyes were flattened against the glass and a mass of bristly pink spotted flesh surrounded them.

The Captain jumped back and shook his fist. "You blasphemous blob, you gelatinous jerk, you galactic gumball. Don't think you can frighten me. I'll sort you out. If I don't get you computerized I'll have you for burgers." Kalmic stood back, stunned by the rage. RAD 33 looked as angry as Captain Aggrow, who was now standing well back and shaking his fist. RAD 33 was the most angry and aggressive life-form she had encountered. It must have been the size of a whale and reminded her of the Sadic life-form which rolls on top of its victims, squashes them, then absorbs them through its skin. "Leave me with it, Captain," said Kalmic. The Captain willingly strode off in a huff.

Kalmic stood still. She looked carefully at the creature behind the thick glass. No-one from this planet had communicated with it before. What a rare chance! It had been here for a month and attacked all advances. She needed to work carefully. She flashed back to her old life-force teacher, Dido, on planet Pluros. "Rule number one. Make sure you're safe. Protect yourself with a screen, bars, wall, shield, forcefield or mental barrier." The words were spoken into her head. The glass was thick. Yes, she was safe.

"Rule number two – remember the life form is feeling frightened or hurt. Forget your own fear and focus on the fear of the other frightened life form. Try to reassure it that it is safe. You are not a threat and you will not harm it." Kalmic looked calmly at RAD 33 and let her arms relax by her sides. She opened her hands to show that she had nothing in them.

"LISTEN, Kalmic, LISTEN!" the words were so clear now it was as if Dido, her teacher, was with her. "The Universe's problems would be solved if we only listened." Kalmic focussed deeply into the six raging eyes of RAD 33. She looked beyond his eyes and into his being. Her head leaned towards the pink blotch body to hear more sounds. She tried to smell the feelings of this creature. Her hands and her body sent out listening messages. What was RAD 33 feeling? What was RAD 33 trying to say? No words were spoken but as they stood there, the 9 year old cosmic kid and the age-old and angry life form RAD 33, communication began. Both were locked, frozen as they connected for the first time on Planet Earth.

Kalmic understood. Alone, trapped in a strange room, on a foreign planet, taken from its own galaxy by intruders while rolling with its family. No food. No food that could be eaten. Where was its fluglemoss, its energy source? Tired of being angry, tired of being frightened, it wanted freedom. Kalmic moved slowly closer to the glass. RAD 33 moved back slightly and flashed its eyes orange and crimson. Kalmic froze. "Remember the angry person has the problem. If you become frightened then you will have a problem too," whispered her teacher.

Kalmic checked her fear. "RAD 33 has the problem not me. He's frightened, alone and hurt." She heard Dido's voice in her head saying, "Acknowledge its problem, Kalmic." Kalmic focussed again and with her eyes, brain and body sent her understanding and feeling for the frightened life before her. Her body vibrated with sorrow and her thoughts were as if she was RAD 33 herself. Her feelings went inside so she felt the fear herself. Her mind let RAD 33 know she knew and shared his pain.

Immediately, Kalmic felt a softening and slight relaxing. The six eyes flashed less and became more pink. RAD 33 eased its flesh off the thick glass and settled back to look more like the handsome blob that he was. He felt understood. Kalmic relaxed a little too, but stayed focussed. "Send your own positive energy, Kalmic," whispered her teacher from the past.

No words came to her but Kalmic imagined her own life force going out and surrounding RAD 33. Like a channel of pink light it moved out from her, through the glass and surrounded RAD 33 in a pink cloud. The eyes became more gentle and sad. The body sagged slightly, went pink and began to flow with moisture. Kalmic recognized a Sadic life form, crying – crying from fear and loneliness. The angry armor had gone. Gently, Kalmic moved to the glass and put her hand on it. A branch-like shape slowly crept out of the blob and touched Kalmic's hand through the glass. Contact!

Kalmic returned early the next day. This time she went straight to Captain Aggrow. She didn't want him upsetting RAD 33. Captain Aggrow was in a fine mood. One of his scientists had made a miscomputation and caused more work. Kalmic hesitated before approaching Captain Aggrow. She heard an echo from yesterday. "Remember the life form is feeling frightened or hurt." Captain

Aggrow afraid? What reason would he have to be afraid or hurt. She approached the Captain cautiously. "So here's the Cosmic Con, huh! Come to play with the aliens, eh? This is not a zoo. My men work with technology. They're experts. Go and suck candy in the tea room, Girlie."

"Listen, Kalmic. The angry person has the problem," urged the echo in Kalmic's mind. Kalmic relaxed. She didn't move, she just looked at Captain Aggrow and her eyes went deep beyond the angry red face. This man has a problem? She searched. Yes, he was afraid. Afraid of Kalmic. Afraid of his own scientists. "Stop staring at me. Stop it! What do you want?" said an irritated Captain Aggrow. "You're frightened," said Kalmic quietly. "Frightened? Me, afraid! Don't be silly! Now what do you want? Stop your silly games."

Kalmic stared deeper still and searched below the angry and fierce face. "You're frightened that your men might be smarter than you. You're frightened I might be able to do something you can't. You're frightened that people might see you're not really big and powerful, but just scared." Captain Aggrow stammered "I'm not, I'm not." His face went white now. No one had talked to him like this before. Captain Aggrow sat down suddenly. Kalmic smiled gently at him and sent him some pink light and left him staring into space.

She walked quietly into RAD 33's room. RAD 33's six sharp eyes saw her immediately and lit up. He didn't move from his place in the middle of his room. Kalmic sent him some more of her pink, friendly energy as welcome. She received a yellow glow back.

Today she would get closer. She turned off the alarm switch on the glass entry door, slowly turned the handle and opened the door. She stepped in. "I have no need to be afraid," she repeated. Clunk, the door slammed behind her. She focused hard on mixing her own feelings with RAD 33's. His six eyes fixed on Kalmic as RAD 33 lifted himself off the floor, paused, then moved slowly towards her. Odd lumps moved in and out from him as he dragged towards her.

"Keep your hope and life force strong, Kalmic," whispered her old friend. Kalmic stood. The lumping shape of RAD 33 moved right up to her. The lumps touched her then moved around her. Her body froze but her head went up as she made sure she had air. The form was right around her now but for her shoulders and head. She smelled the flesh. It was sweet. It was soft. A little clammy, but the vibrations that came through it were of a friendliness and happiness. "Happy for the first time on your planet," he seemed to say without words. "We're together, we know each other's mind and we care." Ripples started inside the surrounding body as if balls were gently massaging her. Kalmic laughed. The balls suddenly jiggled with a kind of laughter too. That night Kalmic wrote her report for the Ministry of Alien Affairs.

Lifeform	From Sadic Family
Movement	Rolling
Food	Vegetation on Pyros
Speak	Universal unspoken language
Attitude	Life-loving, friendly, no wish to dominate or take power over people.
Emotions	Fear, loneliness, sadness, anger, love, hope
Opinion of Earth	People think and use technology more than they feel. Poor communication. Some friendly. Humans like to control one another.
Wish	To return to planet Pyros to continue peaceful existence with family.
Recommendation	Be transported back to Pyros immediately.

Kalmic smiled.

Date _____ Name _____

DEBRIEF

1. Name 2 signs of Captain Aggrow's anger.

_____

_____

2. Name 2 signs of RAD 33's anger.

_____

_____

3. Write down 4 important rules or things to remember when meeting with angry people.

_____

_____

_____

_____

4. What was RAD 33's problem?

_____

_____

5. What are some wise messages that you carry in your head?

_____

_____

6. Can you think of a word from our Earth language to describe what RAD 33 did to Kalmic at the end?

_____

7. What do you think was Captain Aggrow's problem underneath his anger?

_____

_____

8. What do you think is the Universal unspoken language?

_____

_____

9. Say how you would deal with an angry friend or visitor.

_____

_____

10. Draw the Alien RAD 33.

LESSON EIGHTEEN

Cold Water Words

Age Level:

6 yrs. +

Teaching Strategy:

Whole class discussion
Small group activity

Key Concepts:

Other people's anger is their problem.

Materials:

• Worksheet – *Cold Water Words*

Notes:

Most of the exercises in this unit have been about dealing with one's own anger. This lesson is about dealing with someone else's anger without getting drawn into an argument and without escalation of emotion.

Procedure:

1. Distribute copies of the worksheet on p. 63. Discuss the effect of staying removed from other people's anger and not retaliating with more angry words.
2. Ask your students for some ways to cool down a hot situation. Some examples of "cold water" words:
   Yes!
   uh-huh
   Mmmm
   You may be right.
   Does that bother you?
3. Have your students work in small groups to brainstorm "cold water" words.
4. Have each group share their ideas and compile a class list of "cold water" words to be posted in the classroom.
5. Students may also be taught active listening strategies for responding to a friend's anger. In this way, children become resource people for each other as they help each other handle anger in a constructive way. Some helpful phrases:
   It sounds like you're feeling angry/hurt/sad.
   Tell me more.
   That must have made you feel awful!
   You seem to be angry/disappointed/frustrated.
   Let's talk about it.

COLD WATER WORDS

Sometimes other people are angry with us or use put-downs or tease us to try and rouse our anger. Think of some responses that may help to cool down the situation.

63

Grudge Jar

Age Level: 7 yrs. +

Teaching Strategy: Classroom management strategy

Key Concepts: Stating what makes us angry is healthy.
Bottled up anger can become explosive, depressive and bad for health.

Materials:
• A large jar labelled GRUDGE JAR

Notes: This is an idea used by teachers at Colwill School. They found it useful for helping children to get angry thoughts and feelings out of their system. It can be used at home or at school.

Procedure:
1. The teacher has a jar on his/her desk. If a child feels angry about someone or something they write their anger out on a piece of paper, fold it and put it in the jar.
2. At the end of the day the contents of the jar are destroyed.
3. No questions are asked and the contents of the jar remain confidential.

Anger Vocabulary

Age Level:	Word Search One: 6 yrs. + Word Search Two: 9 yrs. + Crossword Puzzle: 7 yrs. +
Teaching Strategy:	Individual activity
Key Concepts:	Stating what makes us angry is healthy. We need to know the words to express anger.

Materials:	• Worksheets – *Word Search One*
	                 – *Word Search Two*
	                 – *Crossword*

Notes:	The following activities are based on the concept that children need to be able to talk about their anger. To do that, they need an anger vocabulary.
Procedure:	1. Discuss the value of talking about our emotions and the value of words to express exactly how we are feeling. 2. Distribute copies of the following activities according to your students' ages and abilities.

WORD SEARCH ONE

```
S  G  T  M  C  R  Y  G  D  N  A  R
H  L  A  U  G  H  Z  M  Q  T  W  M
O  S  D  E  E  E  B  Q  H  R  E  M
U  O  E  I  V  O  L  G  W  X  U  C
T  J  R  I  O  U  I  C  U  G  U  I
Y  P  P  J  L  F  T  E  X  P  S  A
F  Q  M  H  A  F  R  A  I  D  U  K
P  P  A  P  A  Z  Y  M  H  U  G  C
Z  W  T  G  N  T  Q  R  K  H  D  T
L  J  S  W  G  R  E  W  F  I  F  D
U  M  O  G  R  P  C  S  A  T  H  S
B  H  P  Y  Y  U  Z  V  A  O  J  K
M  A  R  O  H  A  X  T  R  X  B  J
```

Find the following words in the maze above. They may go up, down, across or diagonally.

WORD LIST

Afraid	Angry	Fight	Shout
Stamp	Laugh	Cry	Red
Hate	Love	Hug	Hit

WORD SEARCH TWO

```
F O R G I V E X P R E S S
E L P U C E T R O P P U S
E M E M A S B O O K U A I
L A D F R I G H T E N E D
I V O S I X W S E N C O P
N A L A N C X E E S M Z U
G Y P R G D I S T R U S T
S L X C E R U T T A U D
I E E A L B D H T R F L O
E N B S A B I H T U E K W
C O M M U N I C A T I O N
H L O O K E N A S H V R S
S H O N E S T C K C A R B
```

1. Find these words in the maze above. They may go up, down, across and diagonally.
2. Divide the words into two lists:

     'HEALTHY' Communication   'DAMAGING' Communication

WORD LIST

Frightened	Forgive	Sulk
Ask	Truth	Explode
Sarcasm	Feelings	Express
Communication	Distrust	Think
Abuse	Support	Lonely
Punch	Caring	Putdown
Honest		

CROSSWORD

ACROSS CLUES

1. When I feel sad I …

4. I am … of lions and tigers

6. A … makes me feel good

7. Don't …, it hurts

10. When someone teases me I feel …

11. I … my cat

12. When I am angry I could … my feet

DOWN CLUES

2. John got angry and his face went . . .

3. When I feel happy I …

5. If people … someone might get hurt

7. If I get hit it will …

8. I … people who hurt me

9. When I get angry I …

SOLUTIONS

WORD SEARCH ONE

WORD	ROW	COLUMN	DIRECTION
Afraid	7	5	E
Angry	8	5	S
Fight	6	6	NE
Shout	1	1	S
Stamp	10	3	N
Laugh	2	2	E
Hate	2	1	SE
Love	6	5	N
Hug	8	9	E
Hit	9	10	S
Cry	1	5	E
Red	10	6	E

WORD SEARCH TWO

WORD	ROW	COLUMN	DIRECTION
Frightened	4	4	E
Truth	8	10	S
Support	2	13	W
Forgive	1	1	E
Explode	9	3	N
Lonely	12	3	N
Sulk	7	12	S
Sarcasm	5	4	S
Punch	11	2	S
Ask	11	9	S
Feelings	1	1	S
Caring	2	5	S
Communication	11	1	E
Express	1	7	E
Putdown	13	5	S
Distrust	7	6	E
Abuse	10	5	NE
Honest	13	2	E
Think	8	9	SW

CROSSWORD

ACROSS	DOWN
1. cry	2. red
4. afraid	3. laugh
6. hug	5. fight
7. hit	7. hurt
10. angry	8. hate
11. love	9. shout
12. stamp	

Swearing

Age Level:

6 yrs. +

Teaching Strategy:

Whole class discussion
Individual or small group activity

Key Concepts:

Bottled anger can become explosive, depressive and bad for health.
Stating what makes us angry is healthy.
We need to know the words to express anger.

Materials:

• Worksheet – *What Do You Do When You Want To Swear?*

Procedure:

1. Conduct a circle discussion around swearing. Ask: *Why do people swear? Are you allowed to swear? Why do some people not like to hear swearing? Some people think it's OK for adults to swear, but not children. What do you think? What else could we do to release tension when we want to swear?*
2. (Optional) Follow up the circle discussion by distributing the worksheet on p. 71 to students individually or in small groups.

Date _____ Name _____

WHAT DO YOU DO WHEN YOU WANT TO SWEAR?

A lot of people swear when they want to let their anger out. Sometimes it's a quick way of letting out angry feelings, sometimes people swear because they can't think of all the words to express what they are feeling, sometimes they use the swear words they hear from their family or their friends.

A lot of people don't like to hear other people swearing. Parents or teachers might think, "People will think I'm a bad parent (or teacher) if I let my children swear." Others don't like to hear "God" used for swearing.

A lot of swear words are about parts of our bodies and things we do with our bodies. Some people feel uncomfortable with these words. Whatever the reason, swearing can get you into trouble.

One alternative could be to make up your own swear words that won't offend anyone. Can you think of some?

LESSON TWENTY-TWO

Problem Solving

Age Level: 6 yrs. +

Teaching Strategy:

Whole class discussion
Individual activity

Key Concepts:

We need to know what we want and to ask for it.
We don't always get what we want.

Materials:

• Worksheet – *Play Your Own Problem Solving Video*

Procedure:

1. Introduce the idea of using a process to solve problems. Through discussion, work out a process with your students. For example:

   STEP 1   Name the problem.
   Ask: *What is making me angry?*
   How do I want things to be?

   STEP 2   Identify possible solutions.
   Ask: *What can I do about it?*

   STEP 3   Choose a solution.
   Ask: *Which solution will best solve the problem?*

   STEP 4   Act on your decision.

2. Use the worksheet on p. 73 to help students identify the first steps in the process—have them draw a series of pictures to illustrate the problem situation.
3. Encourage children to follow through with the last two steps in the process if they have problems they wish to act on.

Notes:

If children have serious problems you may need to consult with parents or the school counsellor, or work with the child one-to-one.

Date _____   Name _____

PLAY YOUR OWN PROBLEM SOLVING VIDEO

PRESENT

Problem that I feel angry about

GETTING THERE

What do I have to do about it?

FUTURE

How do I want it to be?

Aggroscenario

Age Level:

9 yrs. +

Teaching Strategy:

Small group or individual activity

Key Concepts:

Owning our feelings is healthy and reduces conflict.
Letting others solve their problems is healthy.
Stating what makes us angry is healthy.

Materials:

• Worksheet – *Aggroscenario!*

Procedure:

The worksheet on p. 75 can be used as a role-play, discussion or written activity. Distribute copies to small groups or individuals for discussion and written answers or cut up the strips and give one to each group for role playing.

AGGROSCENARIO!

> How would you handle the situation
> fairly to get what you want without bottling
> or transferring anger?

1. **Characters:** Cody and brothers Ben and David. A parent if needed.
   Scenario: Cody is playing a computer game. Ben and Steve are watching next to him. Ben keeps telling Cody what to do because he thinks he is a much better player. Cody feels annoyed. Finally David interferes by pressing the keys for Cody!

   Who has the problem? _____

   What could you do to solve this? _____

   _____

   _____

2. **Characters:** Dad, Jenny and Steven.
   Scenario: Dad is yelling and banging boxes around in his bedroom. He charges in and yells, "Where's my tennis racquet?" angrily. No-one knows. He then shouts about how untidy the room is, how lazy Jenny and Stephen are and why aren't the dishes done?

   Who has the problem? _____

   What could you do to solve this? _____

   _____

   _____

3. **Characters:** Adam, Richard and Tony.
   Scenario: Adam is much bigger than Richard and Tony and is jealous of them because they are good at soccer. Walking home after school, Adam teases them and calls them names.

   Who has the problem? _____

   What could you do to solve this? _____

   _____

   _____

Anger in the World

Age Level:

10 yrs. +

Teaching Strategy:

Class discussion
Small group or class activity

Key Concepts:

Violence and abuse is behavior. It can be learned and
  unlearned. It is not OK.
Violence has many forms—verbal, ethnic/racial,
  domestic, institutional, etc.

Materials:

• Newspapers

Procedure:

1. Discuss the forms violence can take. Establish through
   discussion that violence and abuse have many forms
   and can be inflicted on anyone.
2. Bring a pile of newspapers into the classroom and ask
   your students to cut out headlines or photos
   reporting violence, conflict or abuse.
3. Divide the children into groups to make collages with
   the clippings or make a class collage. Ask the students
   to group the clippings that seem to belong together
   and print a label for each category they identify.

We Can Make a Difference

Age Level:

10 yrs. +

Teaching Strategy:

Class discussion
Small group activity

Key Concepts:

We are all responsible for stopping violence.

Materials:

• Worksheet – *We Can Make A Difference*

Procedure:

1. Follow up the collage activity with a discussion about what we all can do to stop the violence in the world around us. Although we don't want to make our children feel responsible for other people's actions, we do want to give them a sense of power and a belief in the possibility of change.
2. Divide the students into small groups and ask each to brainstorm actions that they can take to help improve a particular form of violence. Help them to implement their ideas wherever possible, e.g. make posters, write letters, talk to their own families, establish a peer counselling program at school.

Notes:

Children often suppress their feelings of fear, anger and helplessness over world events. Exercises like these will help children to release these feelings rather than repressing them and feeling depressed.

Date _____ Name _____

WE CAN MAKE A DIFFERENCE

PROBLEM

_____
_____
_____

SOLUTIONS

_____
_____
_____
_____
_____
_____
_____
_____
_____
_____
_____
_____
_____
_____
_____
_____
_____

BIBLIOGRAPHY

Everyone Can Win, by Helena Cornelius and Shoshana Faire. Australia, Simon & Schuster, 1990.

Self Assertion for Women, by Pamela E. Butler. San Francisco, Harper & Rowe, 1981.

The Dance of Anger, by Harriet Lerner. New York, Harper & Rowe, 1985.

Your Child's Self Esteem, by Dorothy Corkille Briggs. New York, Doubleday & Co., 1975.

OTHER BOOKS OF RELATED INTEREST FROM NEW SOCIETY PUBLISHERS:

Deschooling Our Lives, Edited by Matt Hern.

Discover the World: Empowering Children to Value Themselves, Others and the Earth, edited by Susan Hopkins & Jeffry Winters.

Dumbing Us Down: The Hidden Curriculum of Compulsory Schooling, by John Taylor Gatto.

Everyone Wins! Cooperative Games and Activities, by Sambhava & Josette Luvmour.

The Friendly Classroom for a Small Planet: A Handbook on Creative Approaches to Living and Problem Solving for Children, by the Children's Creative Response to Conflict Program.

Keeping the Peace: Practicing Cooperation and Conflict Resolution with Preschoolers, by Susanne Wichert.

A Manual on Nonviolence and Children, compiled and edited by Stephanie Judson.

One World, One Earth: Educating Children for Social Responsibility, by Merryl Hammond & Rob Collins.

Playing With Fire: Creative Conflict Resolution for Young Adults, by Fiona Macbeth & Nic Fine.

Teaching Young Children in Violent Times: Building a Peaceable Classroom, by Diana E. Levin.

Who's Calling the Shots? How to Respond Effectively to Children's Fascination with War Toys and Violent TV, by Nancy Carlsson-Paige & Diane E. Levin.

THE ANGER RULES

It's OK to feel angry *BUT*

- Don't hurt others

- Don't hurt yourself

- Don't hurt property

—*DO* talk about it.